MEDIA LITERACY™

HOW POLICY
AND **PROFIT**
SHAPE CONTENT

MEGAN FROMM, Ph.D.

rosen publishing's
rosen central®

NEW YORK

Published in 2015 by The Rosen Publishing Group, Inc.
29 East 21st Street, New York, NY 10010

First Edition

Library of Congress Cataloging-in-Publication Data

Fromm, Megan.
How policy and profit shape content/Megan Fromm.—First edition.
    pages cm.—(Media literacy)
Includes bibliographical references and index.
ISBN 978-1-4777-8064-0 (library bound)
1. Journalism—Economic aspects—Juvenile literature. 2. Online journalism—Economic aspects—Juvenile literature. 3. Advertising—Economic aspects—Juvenile literature.
I. Title.
PN4731F76 2015
070.4068—dc23

2014010970

Manufactured in Malaysia

CONTENTS

INTRODUCTION

Today's news industry is facing a drastically different business model than publishers in the nineteenth and twentieth centuries. Changes in profit margins, advertising revenue, and overhead costs have altered the business model for journalism and other forms of mass media. In turn, the types of content offered and the manner in which it is gathered and disseminated is also different.

In part, many of these changes have been fueled by technological growth and evolution. However, changes in federal communications and business ownership policy have also contributed substantially to contemporary publishing models. News outlets are facing a critical juncture for change with no clear answers because citizen demands and technology are constantly changing.

What used to be a reliable financial buttress for traditional newspapers, advertising has now become a more nebulous form of profit potential. Business managers know they need

At the height of the newspaper industry, publishers relied on retail advertising to bring in the majority of profits. Now, publishers need alternative financial models.

advertising to support news publication, but what kind, and aimed at whom? How do you satisfy advertisers who hope to market to a specific audience when the audience of the Internet is vast and anonymous?

Incidentally, part of adapting to a new financial model for journalism is a shift in expectations, both on the part of advertisers and media owners. The once-predictably lucrative income from classified and retail advertisements has been replaced by an ongoing quest for page views and click-through rates. And because this type of consumer behavior depends on so many largely uncontrollable factors, many news outlets are finding they have to adjust expectations accordingly.

Simply put, today's journalism is often at the whim of market forces, placing journalistic integrity at direct odds with capitalistic enterprise. Consumers and truth remain stuck in the middle of an ongoing and oftentimes ideological tug-of-war between profit and public service.

CHAPTER ONE

CHANGING PROFIT MODELS: FROM PAST TO PRESENT

In the golden age of journalism publishing, most newspapers were family owned. Even major national newspapers, like the *New York Times* and *Washington Post*, were owned by families who had been in the business for decades. But, don't be fooled; these newspaper barons were giants in their own right, and "family owned" should not be conflated with visions of small mom-and-pop enterprises run out of a shop on Main Street.

In his book *The Vanishing Newspaper: Saving Journalism in the Information Age*, author Philip Meyer explained just how out of hand journalism profits had become by the late twentieth century. During that time, many traditional media owners were exorbitantly successful, raking in profits between 15–20 percent any given year, with typical newspaper monopolies in 2001 earning almost 21 percent in profits per year.[1] Comparatively, other retail industries earned roughly 6–7 percent in yearly profits. The cumulative

result of such a profit-driven model is an increasingly worse product, Meyer argued. "That easy-money culture has led to some bad habits," Meyer wrote. "If the money comes in no matter what kind of product you turn out, you become production-oriented instead of customer-oriented. You are motivated to get it out the gate as cheaply as possible. If your market position is strong, you can cheapen the product and raise prices at the same time. Innovation happens, but it is often directed at making the product cheaper instead of making it better."

During the second half of the twentieth century, the breakdown of advertising revenue that supported most newspapers shifted from retail-centric to classified-centric, meaning that by the year 2000, most newspapers were

The *New York Times* (www.nytimes.com) was one of the first major newspapers to institute a paywall, or online subscription service. Newspapers have struggled to make paywalls as lucrative as traditional subscriptions were decades ago.

supported relatively equally between retail and classified advertising instead of relying solely on the former.[2] Classified advertising, which comprises job ads, help-wanted solicitations, and real estate and auto advertising, is less stable than retail advertising because it is subject to greater economic fluctuation.

Combine this reality with the rise of cheaper online advertising and digital publishing models, and many experts predicted the death of traditional newspaper journalism entirely. But, Meyer argued, if media owners can find a way to be comfortable in a more realistic 6–7 percent profit margin, journalism just might survive. The problem, Meyer articulated, is that many traditional media owners just do not know how to adjust their model appropriately. "They know they have to adjust to the reduced expectations that technology-driven change has brought them. They just don't know how," he explained.

NEWSPAPERS STRUGGLE TO ADAPT

In the last decade, the inability of traditional newspapers to adjust to new market forces has led to the shuttering of major newspapers across America. From the *Rocky Mountain News* to the *Seattle Post-Intelligencer* to the *Baltimore Examiner*, newspapers big and small have closed up shop. Some moved online, while others ceased operations indefinitely.

But before they closed their doors, some media companies sought other cost-cutting measures, many of which threatened to sacrifice the very quality and watchdog intent of traditional journalism. These measures included closing foreign bureaus overseas, eliminating foreign coverage altogether, laying off reporters, merging print and digital newsrooms, and relying on wire service subscriptions to fill in the gaps in coverage. While these moves might have been financially necessary, they are in some ways antithetical to the very purpose of journalism.

For example, the shrinking of foreign bureaus means less global coverage of important events. It also means that when and if those events are covered, they are covered only from the singular perspective of whichever news organization happens to have the resources to be on location. According to Jodi Enda of the *America Journalism Review*, eighteen newspapers and two media chains closed every one of their foreign bureaus between 1998 and 2010.[3]

The *Rocky Mountain News*, in Denver, Colorado, printed its final issue in 2009 after it failed to attract a buyer. Denver, a city of almost 650,000 people, now has only one major newspaper.

To reduce costs, ABC has replaced its bureaus in Moscow, Paris, and Tokyo with traveling one-person bureaus in Nairobi and the United Arab Emirates, among other locations.[4] NBC has made similar moves, and in 2013, CNN became the last American TV news bureau to leave Iraq.[5]

"The scaling back in Baghdad is emblematic of a broader scaling back among TV news organizations when it comes to foreign bureaus," wrote Alex Weprin about CNN's decision to leave Iraq. "Expensive offices filled with staffers that only produce a handful of stories a year are going away in favor of correspondents or anchors who fly to wherever the story is on short notice."

INNOVATION: A SILVER LINING

Some journalists see the decline of the traditional economic model as an eventual boon for citizens. In 2007, Slate journalist Jack Shafer argued that the burst newspaper profit bubble was a much-needed reality check for media owners.[6] Thanks to the digital age, Shafer wrote, media owners "need to acknowledge that now that they're no longer the monopoly conveyors of information in their markets, their days of guaranteed 20 percent operating margins are over, and those astronomical valuations of yesteryear were a fluke."

If media owners stop chasing unrealistic profit margins and start focusing on rethinking both the profit and the product, Shafer argued that innovative journalism models just might survive the death of outdated ones. As companies leave the journalism market, Shafer and other journalists have hope that new blood will replace dried up ink and that journalism will revitalize itself in the name of twenty-first-century democracy.

In some cases, Shafer's predictions have come true. Innovative and nonprofit models of journalism are popping up across America, and while many struggle to survive, some are producing quality journalism that capitalizes on digital technology without sacrificing journalistic

Joan B. Kroc, wife of McDonald's CEO Ray Kroc, bequested $225 million to the nonprofit news organization National Public Radio (NPR) upon her death.

integrity. These business are largely supported by philanthropic dona-tions, grants, and advertising.

For example, organizations like the Pulitzer Center and the Center for Public Integrity have taken on the task of reinvigorating investigative journalism for the public good.

Media scholars and critics fear that with fewer journalists around the world covering stories of global importance, the ability of these journalists to maintain their watchdog function is compromised.

"Today, Americans' need to understand the struggles of distant peoples is greater than ever," wrote journalist and foreign correspondent Pamela Constable in the *Washington Post*. "Our economy is intimately linked to global markets, our population is nearly 20 percent foreign-born, and our lives are directly affected by borderless scourges such as global warming and AIDS. Knowing about the world is not a luxury; it is an urgent necessity.... I am convinced that cutting back on firsthand reporting from abroad and substituting cheaper, simpler forms of overseas news delivery is a false economy and a grave mistake."[7]

Some journalists argue that the most significant drawback to today's digital age is more rudimentary than closing bureaus or a decline in international news. Instead, when the forces of supply and demand hit journalism, it's the lack of basic information that will be most harmful for citizens and democracy.[8]

"Consumers today have 'contextual' analysis coming out of their ears," wrote journalist Michael Hiltzik. "What they're getting less of is the hard information—'what's happening'—around which context is built.... The information ecosystem today is a vast edifice of commentary built upon an ever smaller foundation of hard news."

CHAPTER TWO

BIG MEDIA, BIG MONEY

While individual news outlets are scaling back by laying off reporters or hiring freelancers instead of full-time photographers, to say that the media industry is shrinking would be inaccurate. Instead, the industry is coalescing as larger corporations buy out smaller outlets.

This shift toward concentration and conglomeration of media sources means fewer companies now own more of the available media, putting the balance of corporate power on the shoulders of only a handful of media giants.

As of 2014, much of America's media could be traced back to corporate ownership by one of a few mega-media companies: Bertelsmann, Gannett, CBS, Viacom, Time Warner, Comcast, and News Corporation.[9]

Media consolidation is one way of remedying the profit loss many outlets have faced in the last two decades because companies housed under one proverbial roof can share resources, including staffing and

The Time Warner Center in New York City's Columbus Circle boasts the headquarters of one of the world's largest media corporations.

infrastructure. This kind of synergy—the dynamic of groups working together to create benefits that might be impossible for a single entity to achieve—is what drives much of today's media market. But while these media monopolies might be able to maximize profits, their wide and deep hold on the American media market represents a stark shift away from the independent journalism of the past.

Major media corporations add to their holdings in a number of ways, including through both mergers and acquisitions. In a merger, two or more media companies are consolidated into a single outlet. In an acquisition, the media outlet that has been purchased is generally left intact and becomes one of many holdings in a media conglomerate.

MEDIA CONSOLIDATION AND THE FCC

How the Federal Communications Commision (FCC) chooses to regulate media consolidation and conglomeration is currently part of a larger debate on what economic and business model for journalism is best for citizens and democracy. Changes in FCC regulations over the last few decades have greatly influenced the number of companies a media monopoly may own, which in turn, some argue, affects the diversity of voices in the media market.

By law, the FCC must review its media ownership regulations every four years. In 2013, the FCC was considering relaxing one of its regulatory statutes that bans companies from owning both

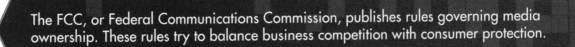

The FCC, or Federal Communications Commission, publishes rules governing media ownership. These rules try to balance business competition with consumer protection.

a radio or televisiom station and newspaper in the same market. According to Reuters, supporters of the ban argued it keeps media monopolies from taking over in smaller markets. But those in favor of the proposed revision said it would allow bigger, more profitable companies the chance to invest in and revitalize a besieged newspaper industry.[10] Due to leadership changes at the FCC, the proposed regulatory changes were shelved and were slated to be revisited.

When considering whether to approve proposals for media concentration and conglomeration, the FCC considers four factors:[11]

RULES OF MEDIA CONSOLIDATION

When media corporations consolidate, they must abide by rules established by the FCC. The FCC is an independent government agency tasked with regulating the communications industry in the United States, including radio, television, wire, satellite, and cable. The agency lists five main objectives on its website:

1. Promoting competition, innovation, and investment in broadband services and facilities
2. Supporting the nation's economy by ensuring an appropriate competitive framework for the unfolding of the communications revolution
3. Encouraging the highest and best use of the [radio] spectrum domestically and internationally
4. Revising media regulations so that new technologies flourish alongside diversity and localism
5. Providing leadership in strengthening the defense of the nation's communications infrastructure

1. The extent to which the combination will increase the amount of local news in the market

2. Whether each media outlet in the combination will exercise independent news judgment

3. The level of concentration in the designated market area

4. The financial condition of the newspaper or broadcast station, and whether the new owner plans to invest in newsroom operations if either outlet is in financial distress

In general, the FCC says it considers media concentration in smaller markets to be more problematic than concentration in larger markets and therefore requires a higher burden of proof before approving media mergers and acquisitions in these smaller communities.

But why, exactly, do some advocates draw such a direct line between media ownership and democracy? Simply put, there is power in diversity and independence—and when power resides in the hands of the few, who will speak for the many?

CHAPTER THREE

NET NEUTRALITY AND THE FIGHT FOR ACCESS

Legislators and media activists are also engaged in another policy fight: the battle for an open and free Internet. At its core, the Internet is designed for equal access and democratic use. In fact, FCC regulations adopted in 2010 were designed to preserve an open Internet, one in which all websites and content have equal potential for access and distribution.

The open Internet regulations were meant to protect the Internet as described by the FCC and as it currently exists: as "a level playing field where consumers can make their own choices about what applications and services to use, and where consumers are free to decide what content they want to access, create, or share with others." These rules, also known as net neutrality principles, were set in motion to preserve these ideals.

If net neutrality principles were no longer the norm, Internet companies could regulate what type of content is provided and at what speed. This would mean a more pay-per-view approach to web surfing.

To better understand what all this means, imagine this scenario that would be possible if the principles of net neutrality are overturned: You go online to watch your favorite television show and opt to stream it over a popular service such as Netflix. The quality is exceptional, with a clear picture, crisp audio, and speedy image buffering. Your Internet service provider knows that Netflix is a profitable, high-traffic site, and it has made sure this site receives premium tech support. Later that day, you log on to your friend's blog, hoping to catch up with her summer of international travel and watch videos of her touring faraway places. Unfortunately, your friend's blog brings in no advertising revenue and offers little profit incentive for your Internet

Comcast Corporation, a major media conglomerate, owns subsidiaries such as NBC Universal and Hulu. CEO Brian Roberts has managed growth of the company to more than $64 billion in annual revenue, according to Comcast's website.

service provider. So, your friend's videos are pixelated, slow to load, and out of synch with the audio. Want better access? You'll have to pay.

Another hypothetical scenario in a world without net neutrality might look like this: Your family uses a service such as Comcast for its Internet service. However, Facebook was just purchased by Verizon, an opposing Internet service provider. Now, if you want to access Facebook using your Comcast connection, you'll have to pay an additional monthly service charge.

THE FCC'S 2010 OPEN INTERNET ORDER

The following three rules comprise the FCC's 2010 ruling to ensure an open Internet and the preservation of net neutrality. The order mandates that Internet providers observe the following standards:[12]

1. **Transparency:** Broadband providers must disclose information regarding their network management practices, performance, and commercial terms of their broadband services.

2. **No Blocking:** Fixed broadband providers (such as DSL, cable modem, or fixed wireless providers) may not block lawful content, applications, services, or nonharmful devices. Mobile broadband providers may not block lawful websites or applications that compete with their voice or video telephony services.

3. **No Unreasonable Discrimination:** Fixed broadband providers may not unreasonably discriminate in transmitting lawful network traffic over a consumer's broadband Internet access service. The no blocking and no unreasonable discrimination rules are subject to limited exceptions for "reasonable network management."

Now, do you see the problem? In short, the opposite of net neutrality is a pay-per-view approach to the Internet. If the principles of open Internet are ignored, Internet service providers can direct resources and support to high-profit, high-traffic sites while allowing independent, low-profile websites to struggle until consumer demand is high enough to warrant better service and faster access.

PROTECTING THE OPEN INTERNET

Unfortunately, major media companies have taken to the courts to challenge the FCC's open Internet rules and the organization's authority to enforce such regulations. In early 2014, a U.S. court of appeals in Washington, D.C., overturned portions of the open Internet rules, ruling the FCC cannot regulate what services wireless Internet providers can offer, at what prices, and to whom.

Slate journalist and open Internet advocate Marvin Ammori minced no words in describing exactly how detrimental this ruling—the result of a court case originally filed against the FCC by Verizon—is for the future of the Internet. "The loss was so definitive, the powers granted to cable and phone companies so outrageous, that the FCC has a live grenade in its lap," he wrote in January 2014.[13]

The 2014 ruling is a complex reaction to the semantics of the FCC's orders and the terminology it uses to characterize and categorize communication carriers. Without getting too technical, the FCC still has a number of options to respond to the ruling and continue its fight for net neutrality, including revising current codes or turning to Congress for more explicit legislation.

As a response to consumer skepticism after the appeals court ruling, Verizon general counsel Randal Milch issued a statement saying customer access will not change in light of the ruling. "Verizon has been and remains committed to the open Internet that provides consumers with competitive choices and unblocked access to lawful websites and content when, where, and how they want. This will not change in light of the court's decision," the statement said.[14]

CHAPTER FOUR

ALTERNATIVE PRESS MODELS

Given the real and significant limitations American journalism is facing in the digital age, some scholars and journalists are looking to alternative economic models to fund hard-hitting, investigative, public-service journalism. Those models include subsidizing news in a way that blurs the lines—somewhat uncomfortably—between government and publisher.

The press in the United States has historically been independent from the government. In fact, the First Amendment of the Bill of Rights guarantees that Congress, the president, and the courts shall not impede freedom of the press. As such, the news industry developed on the streets of capitalism and now faces what some might consider a very capitalistic demise. Demand has waned, so like any other commodities-based industry, journalism is going out of business.

THE BBC ROYAL CHARTER AND AGREEMENT

The BBC is governed by a Royal Charter and Agreement, which outlines six principles of public service:[15]

1. Sustaining citizenship and civil society
2. Promoting education and learning
3. Stimulating creativity and cultural excellence
4. Representing the UK, its nations, regions, and communities
5. Bringing the UK to the world and the world to the UK
6. Delivering to the public the benefit of emerging communications technologies and services

These public purposes form the constitutional rationale for the BBC, and they are what fuel editorial, policy, and economic decisions related to the corporation. Each year, the BBC provides an annual financial report to its license fee payers and Parliament.

Now, imagine if the United States subsidized journalism as a public service, much like the government subsidizes corn or other food staples. This is the model other countries have adopted to preserve journalism in the name of civic engagement and an informed citizenry.

For example, in the United Kingdom, citizens pay yearly license fees for access to BBC News via television, radio, and Internet. Founded in 1922, the BBC's journalistic and entertainment content is funded by these fees. Two operating arms oversee the BBC: an editorial board that manages content and editorial operations and the BBC Trust, which oversees the financial aspects of the corporation.

Columbia University president Lee Bollinger is one of a handful of scholars calling for citizens and journalists to think carefully about the benefits of the BBC's approach. State support does not necessarily mean unequivocal government control, Bollinger argues, citing the true professionalism of the BBC's journalistic arm: "Such news comes to us courtesy of British citizens who pay a TV license fee to support the BBC and taxes to support the World Service. The reliable public funding structure, as well as a set of professional norms that protect editorial freedom, has yielded a highly respected and globally powerful journalistic institution," Bollinger wrote in the *Wall Street Journal* in 2010.[16]

Bollinger likened journalism's need for government assistance to universities' needs for publicly funded research and explained that, in the latter setting, the most rampant instances of abuse have been instigated not from government involvement but corporate abuse. What's more, he considers the influence of corporate advertisers to be just as problematic, if not more so, than a hypothetical government subsidy.

"To take a very current example, we trust our great newspapers to collect millions of dollars in advertising from [oil and gas company] BP while reporting without fear or favor on the company's environmental record only because of a professional culture that insulates revenue from news judgment," Bollinger wrote.

SUBSIDIES: A CONTENTIOUS LIFEBOAT

Bollinger's views, while radical to some, actually highlight a little-known reality: that American news media throughout history has often received some form of public support or government assistance.[17] Scholars Geoffrey Cowan and David Westphal studied the history of public policy and news subsidies and found that postal subsidies for mailing costs of print news media in 2009 were worth $288 million, compared to $1.97 billion in the 1960s. In an interview discussing his research, Cowan explained their findings. "What we think doesn't work is to say there has always been a church/state kind of separation between the government and the press. There just hasn't.

Taxpayer money subsidizes the United Kingdom's BBC network. Governing policies designed to protect public interest help guide the day-to-day operations of the media company.

In fact, there are interesting ways that the government's funding of the news plays against some stereotypes," he said in an interview with Nieman Lab's Laura McGann.[18]

The United States' popular public broadcasting is a perfect example of how subsidies can help buoy quality journalism. In a 2012 public opinion poll, the Public Broadcasting Service (PBS) was ranked the number one most trusted institution supported by tax dollars and was considered the most fair network for news.[19]

Taxpayer dollars also help fund National Public Radio, although such monies make up only a fraction (less than 10 percent) of NPR's total annual revenue.

But government subsidies are not the only hope for propping up the economic foundation of journalism. And some journalists believe they should be left off the discussion table completely, arguing that market forces will do their work and a new kind of journalism will emerge from the ashes. As author Dan Gillmor writes in Salon: "I'm not itching to bail out a business that is failing in large part because it was so transcendentally greedy in its monopoly era that it passed on every opportunity to survive against real financial competition. With a few exceptions, the newspaper industry essentially deserves to die at this point."[20]

Gillmor proposes instead that the government subsidize an Internet infrastructure of high-capacity, wide-open broadband networks: "If we're going to spend taxpayers' money in ways that could help journalism, let's make that benefit a byproduct of something much more valuable. Let's build out our data networks the right way, by installing fiber everywhere we can possibly put it. Then, let private and public enterprises light it up."

Because journalism has historically been exempt from government oversight and involvement thanks to a robust First Amendment protection, government subsidies are a contentious topic and an approach not fully supported by all journalists and media professionals.

One vocal journalist against subsidies is Steve Buttry, digital transformations editor at Digital First Media. After more than forty years in the media industry, Buttry has adamantly expressed his hesitations against government subsidies for American press, arguing that journalists cannot properly serve

National Public Radio is partially supported by taxpayer contributions and provides news and music programming to independent radio stations across the country.

as watchdogs of government if the same government signs their paychecks. His preeminent concern, shared by others, is that government sponsorship would ultimately lead to further government regulation of the media industry, which is contrary to the purpose of journalism.[21]

WHAT IS NEWS WORTH?

FCC regulations, government subsidies, and taxpayer support are all potential answers to a simple yet boding (and as yet, unanswered) question: What is news worth? And perhaps more important: Will readers pay?

To take a wide-lens approach to what the news industry needs to survive means stepping back and realizing that somewhere, in the transition from paper to pixels, readers stopped believing they should pay for news. The new product—an online, ever-changing screen versus a broadsheet newspaper—has become more intangible. The news producers—both professional and citizen alike—have become too numerous to count. And somewhere along the way, these changes translated into perceptions of decreased value for readers.

Websites like the Huffington Post (www.huffingtonpost.com) are testing new profit models for the news.

Instead, news outlets are finding that what citizens were once willing to pay a quarter for every day, and even $1 on Sundays, is now seemingly not worth a $10 monthly paywall fee.

The news about news is not all grim, however. A 2013 study by the Reuter's Institute for the Study of Journalism shows that younger readers are increasingly more likely to pay for news via online subscriptions. Perhaps because these readers, ages twenty-five to thirty-four, have come of age in the era of paywalls, they are less likely to view such finance structures as novelties.[22]

Even still, the future financial model for successful journalism is a moving target. Whether newspapers will go entirely digital, whether international reporting will cease to exist, or whether journalism will even continue to be a full-time profession remains to be determined. What is clear, however, is that the impetus for change lies clearly in the hands of ordinary citizens who realize the value of information in shaping democracy and preserving the qualities of life held most dear in America.

To revisit an old cliché: talk is cheap, but information isn't.

CHAPTER FIVE

WORKING IN NONPROFIT JOURNALISM:

AN INTERVIEW WITH SARAH WHITMIRE, ENGAGEMENT EDITOR AT THE CENTER FOR PUBLIC INTEGRITY

Past journalism experience: Internships with the Center for Public Integrity, *Draft* magazine, *Phoenix* magazine, Ahwatukee Foothills News
Education: Walter Cronkite School of Journalism and Mass Communication at Arizona State University, class of 2011, master of mass communication, bachelor of arts in digital journalism

Did you work in student media in high school or college? If so, how did that prepare you for your current career?
I was a part of the yearbook staff in high school and wrote opinion columns briefly for my college paper. Even though the experience with

Sarah Whitmire is the engagement editor at the Center for Public Integrity, a nonprofit journalism organization in Washington, D.C. In high school, Whitmire worked on her school's yearbook staff.

yearbook was a print media–type operation, it was my first experience working with photo-editing and design software that I now use on a daily basis for web production duties. Being involved in student media can also familiarize a would-be journalist with deadlines, the editing process, and the experience of being a team player.

How do you find story ideas?

My day-to-day job isn't what most would call conventional journalism. It's perhaps a bit closer to marketing or public relations. My main job responsibility is trying to help make our reporting interesting and engaging to our audience. One way I do this is by paying close attention to comments from our readers and trying to get a sense of what aspects of the story resonate with them. For most consumers of news online, leaving a comment represents a fairly strong level of connection to a piece of journalism—this is why I find them to be a great resource for follow-ups to a big investigation that could include impact from the reporting, reactions from key influencers, or just a compendium of public opinion.

A DAY IN THE LIFE OF SARAH WHITMIRE

"With a job entirely based in production and social media, there's no such thing as a typical day! That being said, my 'ideal' day will include two to three hours just for aggregating and posting content to social media (for us, that means Twitter and Facebook), perhaps another one to two hours to work on packaging and posting stories on our website, and once you add a planning meeting or two, that makes a full day.

I like to check my Twitter feed first thing in the morning; I'm not looking to interact with any posts through the center's Twitter account, but meaning to cull through the feed for items the center's audience may find interesting. I like to schedule posts in the morning for the entire day, remembering that I may want to tweak the queue of posts should news break later on.

I also find or obtain art to accompany each of our stories, so sometimes that means tracking down a freelancer on the other side of the world or walking a reporter through the specifics of "fair use" art on the Internet. If there's a major investigation coming down the pipe, I'll also be tasked with coding simple graphs in HTML or JavaScript, or finding and designing pull quotes.

The center's unique status as a nonprofit means that I'll also need to compile web traffic or social media data to (hopefully) show improvement from one grant period to the next. Then lastly, I'll arrange content on the homepage based on importance, popularity with readers, and quality of art."

How do you find the right sources?

Given the center's mission, which is to be a nonpartisan source for investigative news, making sure that our brand only shares stories that are factually accurate and as free from bias as possible is of the utmost importance. On Twitter, where satire, sarcasm, and political bickering reign supreme, this can be difficult. In many ways, I find trusted news sources the same way a journalist did fifteen or twenty years ago: by relying on institutional brands like the *New York Times*, the Associated Press, and the *Wall Street Journal*.

Tell us about a story or project that was especially meaningful for you or your publication.

We actually just published an investigation that was a real risk, both for myself and my organization. It's a look at the next big fracking [hydraulic fracturing] boom in an area of rural Texas known as the Eagle Ford Shale. We experimented with one of these big image, interactive scrolling presentations for the first time, and it was a really big undertaking for our incredibly small department. We don't have a team of full-time news app developers or on-staff photographers, so in many ways the site design was more or less held together with duct tape and strings, but I am still very happy with how it turned out. Innovating in our own way is crucial in showing the world that we don't produce investigative news in a vacuum.

How do you keep up with changing technology and its impact on journalism?

Keeping up with changing technology requires one to be adaptive and a bit fearless, but honestly, that's it. There's no special guide or holy grail for staying current; one just has to care enough to make an effort to find the next best thing. I've tried countless social media platforms that were getting a lot of hype at a certain point in time but stopped using them, sometimes within a week. Changing technology is only daunting to those who have missed an innovation or two and feel left behind as a result. There are many new media "doubters" in my newsroom who are reluctant to join Twitter or don't understand the merit of [news website] reddit because they believe they are fleeting platforms. And they're absolutely right. But unless you play ball on the platform of the moment, you'll have no way of knowing what the next big deal will be. I think the longer one sits out, the harder it becomes to remain current…

What role do you think citizens have to play in being engaged and critical of the information they consume?

All citizens should be educated on current events, at the national and local level. The problem is, there's more news content out there for consumption than there's ever been, and it's certainly not all good. On the flip side, with a discerning eye and basic understanding of search engines, all of that possibly bad content is open to fact-checking. In this hyper-political world, I feel citizens have to be hyper critical of their news sources.

What advice do you have for students interested in media and journalism careers?

If all you want to do is write, push yourself to learn another skill. Whether it's data analysis, basic coding languages, video editing, or social media prowess, entry-level reporting jobs are scarce. If you can offer another strength to an employer, on top of solid journalistic skills, you'll be that much more valuable to them. No one expects an entry-level reporter to also be a professional videographer/photographer/social media superstar, but at this moment in time, the industry is relying on the next generation of journalists to bring new skills and abilities to the profession. Also, blog about something you're interested in. If you're serious about journalism, start a blog immediately. It's incredibly time-consuming but can go a long way in showing future employers that you are serious about the written (typed?) word and know your way around basic online publishing.

ACQUISITION The purchasing of one media outlet by another media outlet, typically larger. The outlet that is purchased in an acquisition is typically subsumed by the buyer.

CONGLOMERATE A media corporation that owns many other media companies—such as newspaper, television, and broadcast—across markets.

CONSOLIDATION Concentrating media ownership among only a few corporations.

FCC The Federal Communications Commission, tasked with regulating the communications industry in the United States.

MEDIA BARON A successful owner of prominent and powerful media.

MERGER The purchasing of one media outlet by another, typically larger, media outlet. In a merger, the outlet that is purchased typically proceeds to operate under its own namesake or with similar staffing and infrastructure.

MONOPOLY When majority control of a market is owned by a single entity, either a person or corporation.

NET NEUTRALITY The principle that all content on the Internet should be equally accessible to all people. Also known as open Internet.

PAYWALL A system that prevents users from accessing content on a web page without first paying a subscription.

PROFIT MARGIN The difference between the cost of running a business and revenue earned from sales.

SUBSIDIZE To financially support.

SYNERGY The dynamic of companies working together to create benefits that might be impossible for a single entity to achieve.

WIRE SERVICE A news-gathering corporation that allows other media outlets to print its content for a fee.

Center for Public Integrity
910 17th Street NW, Suite 700
Washington, DC 20006
(202) 466-1300
Website: http://www.publicintegrity.org
CPI is one of the country's oldest nonprofit investigative news organizations.

Common Cause
1133 19th Street NW, 9th Floor
Washington, DC 20036
(202) 833-1200
Website: http://www.commoncause.org
Common Cause is a nonpartisan advocacy group committed to helping
    citizens have a voice in the political process.

Federal Communications Commission
445 12th Street SW
Washington, DC 20554
(888) 225-5322
Website: http://www.fcc.gov
The Federal Communications Commission is an independent government
    agency that regulates communication in the United States, including
    radio, television, wire, satellite, and cable.

Free Press
1025 Connecticut Avenue NW, Suite 1110
Washington, DC 20036
(202) 265-1490
Website: http://www.freepress.net
Free Press is an advocacy group whose mission is to promote accessible
    Internet, diverse media ownership, and quality journalism.

Pulitzer Center on Crisis Reporting
1779 Massachusetts Avenue NW, Suite 615
Washington, DC 20036
(202) 332-0982
Website: http://www.pulitzercenter.org
The Pulitzer Center is a nonprofit journalism organization that focuses on
    under-reported topics, especially global issues.

WEBSITES

Because of the changing nature of Internet links, Rosen Publishing has developed an online list of websites related to the subject of this book. This site is updated regularly. Please use this link to access the list:

http://www.rosenlinks.com/MEDL/Poli

FOR FURTHER READING

Brock, George. *Out of Print: Newspapers, Journalism, and the Business of News in the Digital Age*. London, England: Kogan Page Limited, 2013.

Downie, Leonard, Jr., and Robert G. Kaiser. *The News About the News: American Journalism in Peril*. New York, NY: Vintage Books, 2007.

Folkenflik, David. *Page One: Inside the New York Times and the Future of Journalism*. New York, NY: PublicAffairs, 2011.

Jenkins, Henry. *Convergence Culture: Where Old & New Media Collide*. New York, NY: New York University, 2006.

Johnson, Clay. *The Information Diet: A Case for Conscious Consumption*. Beijing, China: O'Reilly, 2011.

Jones, Alex. *Losing the News: The Future of the News that Feeds Democracy*. New York, NY: Oxford University, 2009.

Kaye, Jeff. *Funding Journalism in the Digital Age: Business Models, Strategies, Issues, and Trends*. New York, NY: Peter Lang, 2010.

McChesney, Robert, and John Nichols. *The Death and Life of American Journalism: The Media Revolution that Will Begin the World Again*. New York, NY: Nation Books, 2010.

McChesney, Robert, and Victor Pickard. *Will the Last Reporter Please Turn Out the Lights: The Collapse of Journalism and What Can Be Done to Fix It*. New York, NY: The New Press, 2011.

Newton, Eric. *Searchlights and Sunglasses: Field Notes from the Digital Age of Journalism*. Miami, FL: John S. and James L. Knight Foundation, 2013.

Rosenbaum, Steven. *Curation Nation: How to Win in a World Where Consumers Are Creators*. New York, NY: McGraw Hill, 2011.

Uscinski, Joseph E. *The People's News: Media, Politics, and the Demands of Capitalism*. New York, NY: New York University, 2014.

[1] Meyer, Philip. *The Vanishing Newspaper: Saving Journalism in the Information Age*. Columbia, MO: University of Missouri, 2004.

[2] Meyer, Philip. *The Vanishing Newspaper: Saving Journalism in the Information Age*.

[3] Enda, Jodi. "Retreating from the World." *American Journalism Review*, December/January 2011. Retrieved March 6, 2014 (http://ajrarchive.org/article.asp?id=4985).

[4] Dorroh, Jennifer. "Armies of One." *American Journalism Review*, December/January 2008. Retrieved March 6, 2014 (http://ajrarchive.org/article.asp?id=4443).

[5] Weprin, Alex. "CNN Shutters Baghdad Bureau, the Last U.S. TV News Bureau in Iraq." Mediabistro, May 30, 2013. Retrieved March 6, 2014 (http://www.mediabistro.com/tvnewser/cnn-shutters-baghdad -bureau-the-last-tv-news-bureau-in-iraq_b181431).

[6] Shafer, Jack. "When Bad Financial News for Newspapers Is Good News for Journalism." Slate, February 23, 2007. Retrieved March 6, 2014 (http://www.slate.com/articles/news_and_politics/press_box /2007/02/false_profits.html).

[7] Constable, Pamela. "Demise of the Foreign Correspondent." *Washington Post*, February 18, 2007. Retrieved March 6, 2014 (http://www .washingtonpost.com/wp-dyn/content/article/2007/02/16/ AR2007021601713.html).

[8] Hiltzik, Michael. "Supply of News Is Dwindling Amid the Digital Media Transformation." *Los Angeles Times*, February 5, 2014. Retrieved March 6, 2014 (http://www.latimes.com/business/la-fi-hiltzik -20140202,0,1097804.column#axzz2t7ViDU20).

[9] Common Cause. "Facts on Media in America: Did You Know?" Retrieved March 6, 2014 (http://www.commoncause.org/site/pp.asp?c =dkLNK1MQIwG&b=4923173).

[10] Selyuk, Alina. "FCC Withdraws Proposal to Relax Media Ownership Rules." Reuters, December 17, 2013. Retrieved March 7, 2014

(http://www.reuters.com/article/2013/12/17/us-usa-fcc
-mediaownership-idUSBRE9BG15R20131217).

[11] FCC. "Review of the Broadcast Ownership Rules." Retrieved March 7, 2014
(http://www.fcc.gov/guides/review-broadcast-ownership-rules).

[12] FCC. "The Open Internet." Retrieved March 7, 2014 (http://www.fcc
.gov/guides/open-internet).

[13] Ammori, Marvin. "The Net Neutrality Battle Has Been Lost. But Now We
Can Win the War." Slate, January 14, 2014. Retrieved March 7,
2014 (http://www.slate.com/articles/technology/future
_tense/2014/01/net_neutrality_d_c_circuit_court_ruling_the_battle
_s_been_lost_but_we_can.2.html).

[14] Zajac, Andrew, and Todd Shields. "Verizon Wins Net Neutrality Court
Ruling Against FCC." Bloomberg News, January 14, 2014. Retrieved
March 7, 2014 (http://www.bloomberg.com/news/2014-01-14/
verizon-wins-net-neutrality-court-ruling-against-fcc.html).

[15] BBC. "Public Purposes." September 3, 2013. Retrieved March 7, 2014
(http://www.bbc.co.uk/aboutthebbc/insidethebbc/whoweare/
publicpurposes).

[16] Bollinger, Lee. "Journalism Needs Government Help." *Wall Street Journal*,
July 14, 2010. Retrieved March 7, 2014 (http://online.wsj.com/
news/articles/SB10001424052748704629804575324 7
82605510168?mg=reno64-wsj&url=http%3A%2F%2Fonline.wsj
.com%2Farticle%2FSB10001424052748704629804575324782
605510168.html).

[17] Cowan, Geoffrey, and David Westphal. *Public Policy and Funding the News.*
University of Southern California, January 2010. Retrieved March 7,
2014 (http://www.niemanlab.org/pdfs/USC%20Report.pdf).

[18] McGann, Laura. "Separation of News and State? How Government
Subsidies Buoyed Media." Nieman Journalism Lab, January 28, 2010.
Retrieved March 7, 2014 (http://www.niemanlab.org/2010/01/
separation-of-news-and-state-how-government-subsidies-buoyed-media).

[19] PBS. "PBS Is #1 in Public Trust." February 27, 2012. Retrieved March 7, 2014 (http://www.pbs.org/about/news/archive/2012/pbs -most-trusted).

[20] Gillmor, Dan. "Let's Subsidize Open Broadband, not Journalists." Salon .com, June 14, 2010. Retrieved March 7, 2014 (http://www .salon.com/2010/06/14/pay_for_broadband_not_journalism _subsidies).

[21] Buttry, Steve. "Five Reasons Government Shouldn't Subsidize Journalism." *Buttry Diary*, October 30, 2009. Retrieved March 29, 2014 (http:// stevebuttry.wordpress.com/2009/10/30/five-reasons-government -shouldnt-subsidize-journalism).

[22] Reuters Institute for the Study of Journalism. "Paying for Digital News." 2013. Retrieved March 7, 2014 (http://www.digitalnewsreport .org/survey/2013/paying-for-digital-news).

INDEX

ABOUT THE AUTHOR

Megan Fromm is an assistant professor at Boise State University and faculty for the Salzburg Academy on Media & Global Change, a summer media literacy study-abroad program. She is also the professional support director for the Journalism Education Association.

Fromm received her Ph.D. in 2010 from the Philip Merrill College of Journalism at the University of Maryland. Her dissertation analyzed how news media frame student First Amendment court cases, particularly those involving freedom of speech and press. Her work and teaching centers on media law, scholastic journalism, media literacy, and media and democracy. She has also worked as a journalist and high school journalism teacher. Fromm has taught at Johns Hopkins University, Towson University, the University of Maryland, and the Newseum.

As a working journalist, Fromm won numerous awards, including the Society of Professional Journalists Sunshine Award and the Colorado Friend of the First Amendment Award. Fromm worked in student media through high school and college and interned at the Student Press Law Center in 2004. Her career in journalism began at Grand Junction High School (Grand Junction, Colorado), where she was a reporter and news editor for the award-winning student newspaper, the *Orange & Black*.

PHOTO CREDITS